ASHES TO
APPALACHIA

Published 2023 by Tom Tenbrunsel
Title Credit: Molly Pearson
Cover Design: Muhammad Najib Ullah
Cover photo by Abby Ruppert

Digital Formatting by Molly Pearson
Published originally in eBook and Paperback form

DEDICATION

I dedicate this book to The Friends of Carl Sandburg at Connemara, my dear wife, friends and family and to the appalachian storyteller, poet, mon, cook and musician, and maintainer of The Pig and the Acorn blog, Tipper Presley, for keeping beauty and lore of Appalachia before the public every day.

"If I had but one day left, I would Write a poem"

CONTENTS

INTRODUCTION

Ashes to Appalachia represents the very best poetic work of Dr. Tom Tenbrunsel, showcasing 38 of his most profound and imaginative poems to date. It builds on the success of his earlier books, Walk with Me and Picture This, by curating his strongest pieces into one definitive collection.

For over 50 years, Tenbrunsel has brought psychological insight and witty wisdom to his poetry. As a clinician, professor, and keen observer of human nature, he extracts meaning and inspiration from everyday experiences. His uncomplicated style connects with readers from all backgrounds.

In *Ashes to Appalachia,* Tenbrunsel's talent for capturing truth in plain language shines through. Each poem reflects his compassion, humor, and appreciation for the poetry that surrounds us.

Longtime fans will recognize his sincerity and knack for storytelling, which are on full display in this hand-picked selection. New readers will discover a voice that is wise yet whimsical, serious yet funny, simple yet profound.

With vivid photography and accessible language, this collection invites readers to see life through poetry-colored glasses. Each piece takes you on a journey from love to morality, family to faith, social justice to serendipity.

For seasoned poetry readers or those new to the artform, *Ashes to Appalachia* gathers 38 of Tenbrunsel's finest reflections on the human experience into one volume. It serves as the perfect introduction to a one-of-a-kind poetic voice.

Molly Pearson
Writer, Editor, Adventurer

PROLOGUE

Photo poetry entered the scene about the time of Carl Sandburg, when a photographer artist was commissioned to add pictures to Whitmore's poetry. Sandburg added humor to poetry after centuries. I like to think of photo poetry as adding depth to rhyme, and offering visual enjoyment and a new dimension with which to add humor and the perception of motion to the poem. It adds to the entertainment value of the poem without detracting one iota from the mystery hidden amongst the lines. The photo becomes an extension to the poem, titillating the visual senses.

I would try music poetry but then isn't that exactly what songs already are - poetry put to music? For example, I think Bob Dylan is first a genius poet, then a musician. The photo poem, "Lovely Yet Lonely" actually features a famous painting of a famous bronze statue making the alchemy proposal in it that much more tangible to the reader.

My point is exactly that of John Michael Flynn when he says damn the effete erudites, photo poetry is a growing medium of poetic expression and is here to stay. Being an amateur photographer and a poet, I am in my glory. Enjoy!

ABOUT THE AUTHOR

A writer and a poet, Dr. Tenbrunsel enjoyed a long successful career in Clinical/Sports Psychology. Born and raised in Nashville, Tennessee, Tom graduated from Bellarmine University, obtained his doctorate from St Louis University in 1969. He taught, published and was in administration at Michigan State University and VP for Advancement at the University of Alabama at Huntsville. He is a champion of conservation and has been a board member of The American Chestnut Foundation and Land O' Sky Trout Unlimited. He and his wife reside in the Appalachians of Western North Carolina. They have three successful children and eight grand grandchildren. Dr T. enjoys photography, writing, gardening, cycling, hiking, camping and stalking the elusive trout. His writings and publications speak for themselves. He was selected as a Carl Sandburg Writer for 2023.

Other books by Tom Tenbrunsel include: Casual Gardening, Poetry on My Mind; The Fund Raising Resource Manual; Walk With Me; Picture This; Psychological Self-Help Series (to be released in 2025), My Wrinkle in Time: My Memoirs (work in progress).

Follow Tom online for his latest weekly photo poetic posts at www.tenbrunsel.com

THE ROAD LEAST TRAVELED

Which road? Which? Which shall I take - or not? The eternal question each of us face, now, time and again. Yogi had the simplest, perhaps the best solution. In his wisdom Yogi Berra said, "If you come to a fork in the road; take it!" There, dusting my hands, problem solved.

Robert Frost, one of my all time favorite everyday poets, wrote "The Road Not Taken." Hummmmmm? Regret? Should I have? Oh well.

Scott Peck scribed the NY Best Seller, "The Road Less Traveled: A New Psychology of Love, Traditional Values, and Spiritual Growth." Written decades ago, I think it's most relevant in today's confusing world of questionable values and strange definitions of love. And Lord knows the Spiritual nature of the human is oft wanton. Read it.

My "The Road Least Traveled" poem is but a short insight into my Epiphany one day whilst cycling, in the spirit of Frost, but with the straightforward clarity of Yogi.

"I took the road familiar,
And traveled ne'er so far,
I took the road least traveled,
And found who am, I are!"

Poetry on My Mind, p43

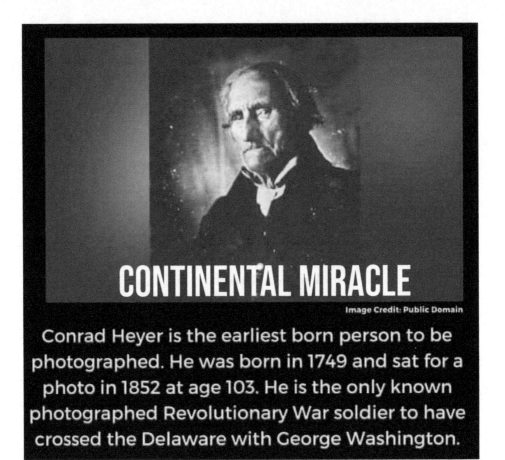

CONTINENTAL MIRACLE

Image Credit: Public Domain

Conrad Heyer is the earliest born person to be photographed. He was born in 1749 and sat for a photo in 1852 at age 103. He is the only known photographed Revolutionary War soldier to have crossed the Delaware with George Washington.

From the depths of Valley Forge, an army all but defeated and scattered, there arose champions of LIBERTY of what was to become the pivotal battle of greatest Nation on earth

The Continental Miracle
There I was
Dead of night,
Sleepless
  Sick
    Starving
In my plight.

Rag-tagged
I knew not yet the Nation,
My shoulders bore,
Clothes stuck to my skin,
Feet bare, bleeding,
Frozen and sore.

I helped push the long boats
In Delawared ice,
Then picked up the march
Of miles,
  'bout twenty,
No news from home
With mere script for money.

Alls that had wintered,
On sock-soup engorged,
Patriots we gathered
To follow George

We slugged and shivered.
We trudged bloody slush,
Passing men,

Exhausted-Fallen
In their tracks,
Sick-starvened
   to death.

We passed a homestead,
Thank God they were Patriots,
For our only hope,
Was to surprise
the dastard Hessians.

Our Journey's end,
The enemy in sight,
To our soul's delight,

The British had party-ed
Drunk,
Christmas Eve night!

SURPRISE!
It was,
The canons roared in place,
The sudden onslaught of battle,
With saving grace
We routed them fleeing,
We overtook them,
    scorned,
Thru the miracle at Trenton,
A Nation was born.

Author's Notes: OK. For those that know history. Washington's Continental Army was defeated, retreated, stuck in God-forsaken bitter winter's Valley Forge.
Many cold, sick, hungry, tattered freezing troops had left, given up, for home.
Washington couldn't pay them. Those few that stayed, numbered in the low hundreds. It would take a miracle of bravest proportions to do what Washington knew he had to do. As they hunkered around open fires, Washington addressed the men, asking them for the unthinkable. He asked them, it our last Solar Minimum, to take up arms, cross the frozen Delaware in wooden long boats, called Durham Boats. Most without boots or proper coats, rags for gloves, mustered what strength within and followed their General twenty plus miles that moon-less darkened night in blood stained slush and freezing rain, dragging heavy horse drawn caissons over hilly terrain, crossing two tributaries, past but one, thank God, one patriotic house, where Washington left guards to assure the SURPRISE he needed to catch the British crack Hessians brigade at Trenton Off guard. He (and God) managed by miracle to line the canons down Main Street, Trenton.
When the canons fired right down Main Street and cross-fired down East Street the British were caught in the hellfire of canons, with their pants down, so to speak, as Continental Troops poured into town overpowering the unprepared Hessians.
The enemy was quartered and Washington's soldiers were allowed no plundering, just boot gathering and left over Turkey and ale.
After negotiating to never fight again, the Hessians were escorted out of Trenton. Trenton was strategic and Washington went on to win the Revolutionary War. The Hessians, true to their word, settled westward, in Hot Springs, North Carolina, never to fight again. It was considered a miracle by Washington, a gutsy move by men to whom we owe our Liberty - Thus the poem.I dedicate this poem to Bill Forstchen for his historical inspiration.
Tom tenbrunsel
Poet Laureate of My Domain

THE APPLE

The Apple may it be,
The Apple you see,
Falls unscrupulously
    From the tree,
And tho it be,
It falls upon I and thee.

For tho we were not there,
That unscrupulous day,
To participate in an unscrupulous way,
Still we were rendered mortal,
By that infamous Apple,
That Apple in the tree,
That Apple as it were,
That Apple was not free.

Would you have partaken,
From that naughty Apple?
Would you have bitten,
From such temptation?
To be smitten,
    Doomed,
As it were to mortal nakedness,
To spend your days,
Covered in cape?
Huh? Would you?
Would you have bitten?
And risked being smitten?

Hindsight is,
It's the devil's playground,
"Jess one little bite,

Z'all it takes,
To be smart and bright,
As He,
    You see,
For goodness sakes,
Just bite!"

You think it was really an Apple?
An apple Apple tree?
I mean I'd of had my eye on Eve!
Now that, satan,
Would of fooled me!

But just like that,
In a touch of nonsense,
Poor ole' Adam,
Made his choice,
He lost a rib,
Was duped by a fib,
When all of that,
Could of been free,
For him, you and me.

So take a lesson,
From the garden son,
Take a lesson from me,
Don't be fooled by what you have,
For what they say could be,
Dance wit Him what brung you,
And don't go a'near,
    That Apple tree!

Questions? Did the Apple fall far from the Tree? Was there just one apple on the Apple Tree? Did both bite, or just one of them? Did they finish the Apple? What kind of apple was the Apple? What happened to the Apple? Who was to blame? Did Adam yell out, "Apple Core, Baltimore," or, was he to ashamed?

Let me ask a question I have pondered: What sort of thing, being, "snake" or whatever could have ever convinced a perfectly pure woman created in the IMAGE of God, in the Garden of Eden prior to ever sinning, to eat the Apple? Did she recognize it? Snakes don't talk. Who was it? And why on God's perfect Earth, would she believe such a thing/being, and take a bite? Have you yourself ever seen such a being/person/ demon? Have you ever been convinced by the devil personified, to do something against God's nature/command? To take a bite? Hummmmmm? Think about it. Things are not always as they seem. Stay alert, do diligence and pray to the Lord God Almighty to deliver you from evil, should it be convincing you.

MY HEART

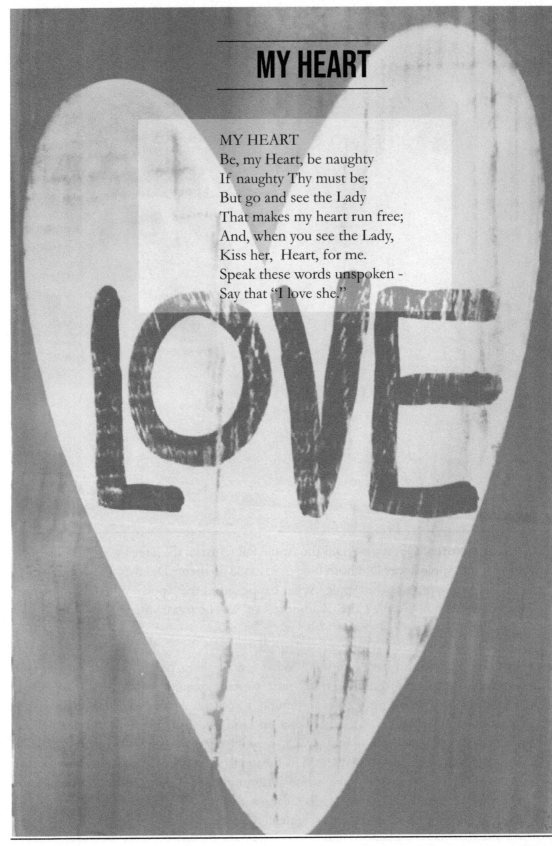

MY HEART
Be, my Heart, be naughty
If naughty Thy must be;
But go and see the Lady
That makes my heart run free;
And, when you see the Lady,
Kiss her, Heart, for me.
Speak these words unspoken -
Say that "I love she."

OH CHRISTMAS TREE

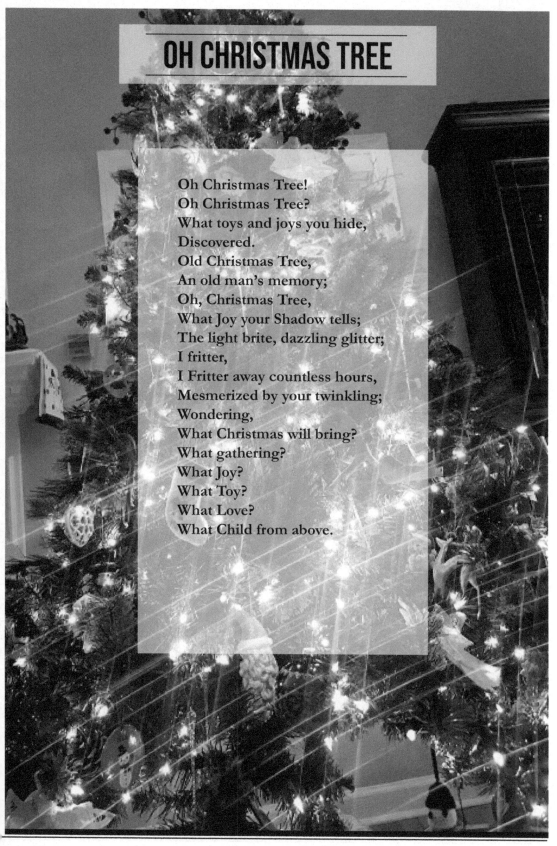

Oh Christmas Tree!
Oh Christmas Tree?
What toys and joys you hide,
Discovered.
Old Christmas Tree,
An old man's memory;
Oh, Christmas Tree,
What Joy your Shadow tells;
The light brite, dazzling glitter;
I fritter,
I Fritter away countless hours,
Mesmerized by your twinkling;
Wondering,
What Christmas will bring?
What gathering?
What Joy?
What Toy?
What Love?
What Child from above.

WOOD OR KNOT

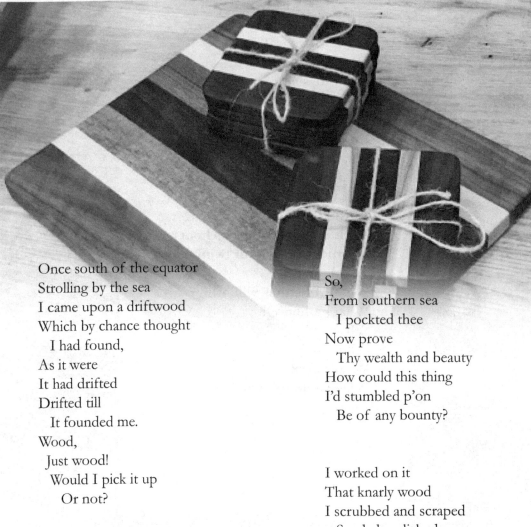

Once south of the equator
Strolling by the sea
I came upon a driftwood
Which by chance thought
  I had found,
As it were
It had drifted
Drifted till
  It founded me.
Wood,
  Just wood!
    Would I pick it up
      Or not?

A knarly thing
Weather bleached
  And rounded
It beckoned me,
  "Pick me up"
I did and mused
What shall I make
When I get back
  To Shop.

So,
From southern sea
  I pockted thee
Now prove
  Thy wealth and beauty
How could this thing
I'd stumbled p'on
  Be of any bounty?

I worked on it
That knarly wood
I scrubbed and scraped
  Sanded, polished.
I'd never, Wood,
Have worked so hard
    Indeed so hard before
In such feverish fit of fury,
  Guess I simply was not over
    My man lost to war.

And I was driven
   Driven,
      Driven,
To find just out why,
Why?
This beastly wood that drifted by,
   Drifting, caught my eye.

Suddenly,
As I worked on it
The answer popped
   Before my very eyes\
I stood back consumed
   Sobbing tears
      Broken down I swear,
It's drifted beauty

Now understood,
   I sighed…

Neither Ash nor Oak
No pine 'twas not
That heart-shaped wooden knot
Reached out
   In captured art
      To so consume my soul,
The wood was
      Purple Heart!*

*Purple Heart is a purplish wood found in Brazil

GAITHERS GARNER

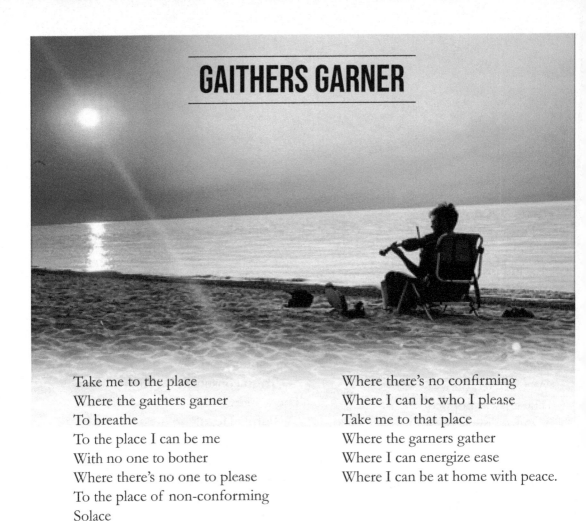

Take me to the place
Where the gaithers garner
To breathe
To the place I can be me
With no one to bother
Where there's no one to please
To the place of non-conforming
Solace

Where there's no confirming
Where I can be who I please
Take me to that place
Where the garners gather
Where I can energize ease
Where I can be at home with peace.

Author's Note: What place is this? Where is this place? And how does one get there? Is it outside or inside - the mind, soul or body? Is it a place needed or not? Possible? Or possibly not? Or a state of mind, wherein to hide? Why go there? Who gather there? Why? Have you been there? Would you like to go? To where the gaithers gather.

This poem is an example of how a concept, "gaithers gather" hit me in the middle of the night. Two words rhythmically jostled about pestering me in my pre-sleep mind. I had absolutely no idea what a gaither was. I sprung into action at my night darkened desk and fleshed out this poem. Next day, I googled the meaning and, ah ha, went back and tweaked the poem.

Write when the concept hits you. Write it right then. Jot it down before the spirit who moved you to poem, exits, and all is lost. The poet gives voice to the spirit.

LEAN-TO LENNY

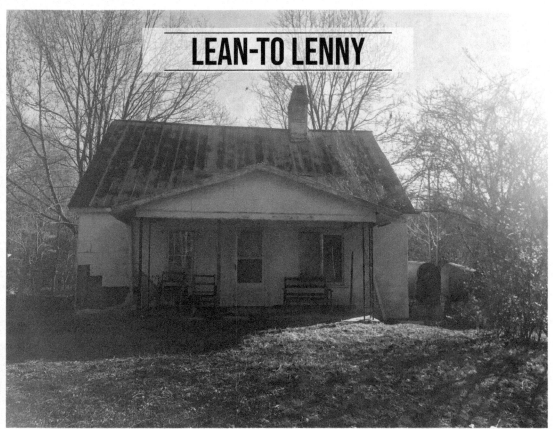

When I pass by,
Up Union Hill,
I know he's inside,
Peering,
   Peeking,
     Silently Still,
Wondering whom am I.

I wave.
He never shows himself,
Just a shadow,
   Of a guy,
But when I return.
He has left me a token,
   On the post.
Somewhat of a ghost.

Lonely?
   Maybe?

Alone man.
A lone house stands.

It's our way of,
Staying in touch,
And saying,
"Hi!"
As I pass by.

Last week,
No token I spied.
The old man,
Died.

I cried.
For I had lost a friend.
In need,
In deed,
Indeed.

Author's Note: Who was the old man?

21

INTO THE FOREST

What does the forest hold,
Dark, deep dark, in her clutches?
What makes me want to venture,
   Yet give pause,
Among towering monsters,
    And who knows what?.

There's a pathway of sorts,
        I take it,
Yet it too, ends abruptly,
Dissipates into nothingness,
Instantly I'm lost.
I thought,
    "Should I go back?"

Suddenly!
    What the heck?
The forest has no exit.

Shadows abound,
There are things around,
Scurrying,
Creeping and crunching,
I shiver and start,
    At pitchness of dark,
But for the sun's peeking
      Through branches.

Who's there?
I want to ask,
But not draw attention,
I creep softly quietly
    Along no path a'tall.

"Who goes there?"
A voice echoes,
    (Or though, I thought),
Perhaps just an owl,
    Or not?

A huff and I imagine,
    A bear or such,

Perhaps some
    Prehistoric clan,
      Or a Sasquatch Man.

I venture further,
Being careful
    Not to get lost,
I bend a twig here and there
Along my would be path.
Yet I turn around,
And no bent twigs,
    I found.

Wearily!
    Mysteriously!
I trudge, what seemed a lifetime,
Of blackened
Forest secrets
    Only,
      Suddenly,
To pop out,
As if through some magical portal,
Whole again,
On the other side,
    Alive,
And renewed
    In the light.

Author's Note: Life, light, darkness and the other side. Light to dark to light. Is it a description of life's journey or just a wild tale of being a bit lost in a deep dark forest? Definitely surreal, as things just don't seem right at times, creatures abound around, no pathway, no trail markings, no guideposts to help the trekker along. You're on your own. You can't go back, only forward. Then, without warning a portal appears and you step through; your journey ended. Amen.

photo by me ☺
Poet Laureate of My Domain

A BOAT WITHOUT A TILLER

A boat without a tiller,
Adrift on an aimless sea,
My mind in endless wonder,
That was me; that was me.

I'm a sail without a boat.
Aimlessly afloat,
Sailing here and high above,
A wild horse without a rope.

How can I ground myself,
Gather friends around my oar,
    To float,
To float my aimless boat,
    Once more,
To heaven's earthly shore.

I knew about the North Star,
But I couldn't steer,
No voice that told me right from wrong,
A voice I couldn't hear.

I flayed and floundered,
There, here and about,
Asking the Lord,
"Lord help me out."

I heard a voice,
I swear on high,
"You have a choice,
Use it wise,
I gave you tools,
To right your boat,
Fix the sail,
Once more to float."

Ice is nice,
So is Fire,
To quench this thirst,
It takes desire.

So git up off,
Your thronely butt,
Go right what's wrong,
'Fore bubbles bursts!

Author's Note: Comments? Questions? Opinions? Ideas? Requests? Likes? Poetry? What did this poem mean to you personally?

MESSAGE FROM THE CHESTNUT

As sure as Frost upon the virus lay,
The Tree will stand supreme again one day;
Though time may toll beyond our mortal means,
The Chestnut will again adorn the country scene.
For lo, these mortals will come to plant and spade,
And cultivate the chestnut day by day,
And return it will upon this hallowed ground,
For it once was dominant and renowned.
But just as weak as we all are too,
So does the Chestnut keep growing shoots anew;
And its persistence is supreme insight,
Lest we not persist and shrivel from a blight.

by Tom Tenbrunsel

The message is quite clear. It's a message to all of us to heed the plight and persist in matters which oft appear hopeless in life. That message is perhaps more relevant than ever in these times. What is remarkable is most people miss the fact that Robert Frost wrote "Evil Tendencies Cancel" in 1936 predicting the parasite (discovered in 1946) that "ended" the blight:

Evil Tendencies Cancel
by Robert Frost - 1936

"Will the blight end the chestnut?
The farmers rather guess not.
It keeps smouldering at the roots
And sending up new shoots
Till another parasite
Shall come to end the blight."

At Michigan State University I had the pleasure on working with Drs. Dutch Weilich and Dennis Fulbright, to help fund their groundbreaking research to return the true American Chestnut (Castania dentata) to it's dominant position throughout the Appalachians. I also served on the board of The American Chestnut Foundation. It's where I met "Mr. Chestnut," Herb Clabo, resident historian and expert advocate of the American Chestnut in the Great Smoky Mountains National Park.

The American Chestnut was the major source of wildlife food in the forests. It's tannic acid was the basis of the tanning industry. It was the source of railroad ties because it didn't rot. Look carefully at the real weathered fence posts in Appalachia. They will be chestnut because they last forever. Many of the trail marker posts along the Appalachian Trail are age-old chestnut. I lived in a house on Bellwood Avenue in Cincinnati that had chestnut woodwork.

There were two factions within ACF research on how to restore this amazing giant of a tree which dominated the eastern United States sometimes 15 feet wide at the trunk and often 100 feet tall: Ours was to restore the tree by discovering a way to defeat the blight with the parasite (virus), just like Frost prophesied; the other was to cross breed the American Chestnut with a disease resistant chestnut. The latter won out and one can purchase disease resistant trees. The new strategy to save the once majestic American Chestnut (very tasty if roasted on an open fire) is to increase the supply and demand for this delicious food source. It is a favorite among chefs. The restaurant may indeed save the Chestnut
Tom Tenbrunsel
Poet Laureate of Castania dentata

LEEWAY: THE SHIPBUILDER'S SECRET

A boat creaks and lurches,
Boards moan and bitch,
　　'ginst the mighty sea,
It is the lurch and creaking that saves her.
It is a well built flexing flagship,
　　That discovered America.
America has survived the same way.

Give and take,
　To and fro,
　　Side to side,
The ship must go,
To resist its crumpling,
　　'ginst the sea
So also,
　You must go,
　　With the flow.

Tall buildings sway,
　They're made that way,
Wings on a plane,
　Flex away.
Strength is deceiving,
Nothing is stand-stillian!
The car leans and lurches,
　　Slides, slips and drifts,
On unrelenting track.
　Heel and toe,
　　Are the combination,
That makes the curve,
　　Seem straight.
You must turn left,
　　To go right,
Confusing?
　It's the,
　　Same on a bike.

The batter's entire body,
Flows with the swing,
In one instant unwinding,
Then CRACK!
Opposing forces,
Give the ball,
New beginning.

Awakened from sleep,
We defend our country,
To re-rite.
A revived,
Constitution,
In a new direction,
Once more,
Ingenuity,
Has beat,
Failed insurrection.

So who did it?
Who thought,
Who thought,
Of such things?
The give and take,
Of the hull,
And the flex-wing,
For goodness sake?

It was Gods will,
As He forged the tools,
And handed them to mankind,
To rite the ships tall,
To rite wrong,
And to make it right
For all,
Praise God's gift,
Ye Patriots,
Ye God-given, Patriots all!

Author's Note: God didn't intend for us to stand-stillian. The Universe was set in motion with God's hand and likely a huge BANG! Of which the roar continues, ever expanding outward. Afterall, ask yourself, what's on the other side of the Universe? But just as important is the need for motion, flexibility in all we make and do. To be rigid is to be left behind. We must explore and build things to withstand exploration. As we must be resilient in our exploring. God gave us the tools to do with. Fear not for God provides leeway so we may find our way on the great ship of life. Let us go forth and do. And in the process figure out, that we must do, to protect what is good. Amen.

*photo public domain of the Nina, the Santa Maria and the Pinta lumbering, lurching, leaking and creaking toward God's chosen America. We were never really lost, but now we're found, were blind but now we see ♪♫♪

BAGGER, YOU AND ME

But the memory is as clear,
As that moonlit night,
We played golf,
At Hampton Cove,
I believe, quite near.

We had started late,
We were the last to tee
We figured we'd get in nine,
The game was golf,
You with me,
We didn't care what time.

I can't remember,
What time it was,
As we, bags shouldered,
Addressed the tee,
It was just the two of us,
And Bagger made it three.

Not sure how many,
Holes we played,
As evening turned to dusk,
Don't even think we payed.
We played thru four or five,
I think?
At six I said "I No can see,"
As I approached a pitch dark tee.

We laughed and hooted,
As the nearby owl could see,
I peeked into sheer darkness,
Without honors,
    It was my turn to tee.

You had blasted one into total darkness,
That ball was never found.
I got all of mine, too.
With my trusty three wood wand.

We looked at each other laughing!
My first son and me,
There was no light left,
That night,
So we walked it in,
    Together,
You and Bagger and me.

Author's Note: A GOLF STORY

My son, Kevin, is a par golfer. I try to stay as close to the fairway as possible, so's I'll get invited back. My best score ever was at Cherokee in Atlanta the Thursday before my daughter's wedding, to the love of her life. At the par five 15th hole I was holding my own, in our threesome: Mr. Wiggins president of the Club, Ray Hansen, my lifelong friend and a par golfer himself (except that day). I'll never forget the moment. I had hit well off the tee and after a second shot, figured I'd play it water-safe and lay up with three, then cross the pond in four to the green. WHEN! Here comes, Buford, our 70 year old fore-caddy, straight at me, holding my 3 wood horizontal in outstretched hands, looking me straight in the eye, proclaiming, "We didn't come here today to lay up."

With Buford's confidence/challenge (in one day, the man knew more about me than myself), I got all of that 3 wood and hit the green in three. Buford was my Bagger Vance.

Buford's words echo in my mind to this day. I wasn't put on this earth to lay up! Oh! and I broke 100 for the first time that day.

*5/7/2020 Written the night "Poetry on my Mind" was published! That's Will in the photo. He started early at Robert Trent Jones Trail, Hampton Cove. Today my oldest grandchild is a scratch golfer

REBIRTH OF MY NATION

I sit at my lonely,
Familiar desk,
Caught up in the whirlwind,
That whisks me along
With it,
Willingly at best.

As no man is an island,
Goodness and patriotism,

Are glue,
Irregardless of race, or ism,
This assimilation has a,
Unique hue view.

It may be my Winter,
But I've planted my feet,
thanks to Yogi,
It ain't over till,

It's over,
I will not retreat.

Worried in darkness,
Ecstatic in the Light,
I am overjoyed,
That WE won,
Barr none,
With brilliant stinging fight.

A plan comes together,
And I am an intricate part.
Every drop of blood shed,
Deserves a Country-altar,
To support the weight,
Of,
Who fought so fiercely,
Their neck's at stake,
Now it's my turn,
To take,
Fearless participation,
In the glory,
Of a Nation,
From within, scorned,
Reborn!

Let Freedom ring from,
Tower and Steeple,
Our government,
Once more,

Of, For and By the people.
Let us share our freedom'
With all on Earth,
For God returned,
A new Liberty,
In my Nation's rebirth.

How lucky am I,
To have been at this
Precipice,
To have witnessed history,
Victoriously gloriously, profound,
Found in God's grace.

United we stand,
Divided no more,
We've rid ourselves,
Of Curly and Moe.

And to the Republic!
One Nation indivisible!
With Liberty,
And Justice,
For all.

Amen.

*"Soon! Very soon now," the
prophet said.

Author's Note: The Photo is of the Old Courthouse in St Louis Missouri where the Dred Scott civil rights decision trial took place in 1846. Dred and his wife, Harriet, petitioned the court for freedom from enslavement. An all white jury of men voted unanimously in their favor; But one shinning example, of the strength of Liberty in this great Republic of ours. We are one Nation under God, Indivisible! Patrick Henry proclaimed "Give me Liberty or give me death!" I agree us
HAPPY FOURTH to all y'all

THAT THESE MEN SHALL NOT HAVE DIED IN VAIN

I came by a man
Kneeling
On hallowed fodder
Praying
Praying for his forefather

I listened quietly
Unnoticed
Silent
As the man spoke
Not of hardship
And grief
But of thanksgiving
That a nation
Was reborn out
Of strife
And
Suffering
And gruesome death

He thanked God
For watching over
His chosen Nation
He remembers
His heritage
He remembers slavery
And on one knee
He remembers
That once brother
Fought brother
That both could be free.

The man
Dressed in his great
grandfather's
Uniform

Out of respect
Prayed thanksgiving
And thanked God Almighty
That his kin
Died a free man!

The man rose
And looked

Right through me
You see I had died
Beside his kin
Me and my soldier brother
Shoulder to shoulder
Soldiers
Both to be reborn again.

Author's Note: History can be changed but not the facts. No slave fought in the Confederate Army. General Lee proclaimed that every black man that signed up for his army MUST first be freed. General Grant paid $400 to the slave owners who brought their slaves to sale to his army. Note, the Emancipation Proclamation wasn't signed by Lincoln until three years into the war. To the righteous, I say look within and repent and unite in one nation under God for, by and of the people, that this nation shall not perish from this earth.

I rewrote Lincoln's words to include, not hinder, that a civil war was fought over states rights. Slavery was on its way out - both black slavery and the enslaved indentured Irish. It had run its course among both North and South. That all men were created equal had persevered from our foundation. Unfortunately, black and white slavery, indentured servants of socialism are rampant yet, in this world Today. The work of the hand of God is yet unfinished. In His name, we pray.

Addendum: Likewise, there are those who say the Civil War was never officially over because there was never a congressional declaration of such or a treaty. To those, I say, let it go. When brother fights brother, there is no need for a treaty. A handshake, a hug will suffice And would be nice. When at Appomattox Lee handed Grant his sword, there was surrender. When Grant handed it back to him, there was the understanding - This is over. Go in peace. Let it never happen again among a people United. Let it go people. We have much bigger fish to fry.

Let Memorial Day remind you of our responsibility to live and prosper together, that brave American souls shall not have died in vain. Peace be with you!

LEXINGTON GREEN

It all started on Lexington Green, preserved to this day as hallow ground. We the people once stood firm against tyranny. April 19, 1975 was the shot heard round the world when a British regular accidentally discharged his rifle and the Revolutionary War was on. It was the birth of a nation. It was Paul Revere's famous ride - one if by land, two if by sea. It was by land as the British faced the Minutemen of a new Nation, under God, that first skirmish lost by the revolutionaries, by we the people, who, outnumbered, were routed only to regroup time and time and time again, against insurmountable odds, to fight and die and persevere, that we the people may be free today. Cherish and protect your freedom.

Let us not forget those brave men who faced imminent opposition on their town greens, fought for our Liberty, and won. We thank you Brave souls, in God's name. Amen.

GITCHEGUMEE

We sailed our ore boat
East toward storm
She twist'd and she creaked
From dusk toward morn
The big lake angry
'Twas rough indeed
Rough as sin
But for "fifteen more miles"
Our families morn
The Three Sisters did us in.

Tom Tenbrunsel
Carl Sandburg Writer 2023

Author's Note: Loving Gordon Lightfoot's song and the legend of the Edmund Fitzgerald, this poem is a snapshot of that tragedy. The photo is of a piece of driftwood I picked up out of Lake Superior on a family trip there once. The driftwood reminded me of The Three Sisters (a series of three gigantic waves) that broke simultaneously onto the deck of the Fitzgerald, probably sinking the ore laden boat.

LOST IN THE WOODS

Lost in the woods,
Alone,
Quiet,
Life fading,

Stillness
Invisible,
Darkening,

Strange and,
Elusive,
But for fleeting glimpses,
of my trusty steed.

Am I really me?
Homeward bound,
Yet at home here too

Arthor's Note: I tweaked it a bit. And will put it in my "Book of Poems." Read the poem slowly, pausing to listen. Don't miss the subtle transition. It's about adventure, about life, about the beauty of being one with nature, about exploring who we are, about solitude, about the journey, about death and life after death. The rider likely had an accident or perhaps a heart attack. Note the angle of the camera is from the rider's perspective, suspended in fleeting transition. The bike, still there (waiting where he "left it" when it happened), the rider/writer, invisible now, writing (still a part of nature) from the grave? "Am I really (still) me," the writer asks, transitioning thru that unknown moment of life to death? Puzzled, exasperatingly rubbing his/her hands over her/his face and hair, the rider, "glimpsing" back at the bike (representing life's passion, life's journey), thinks aloud, "It, it feels so different - dead but, but still alive?" Where is the rider? Where is home? Do life experiences, memories, exist beyond death? Of course. Does a bear scat in the woods? - Tom Tenbrunsel.

The poem was inspired by Troy Carr, a long time friend on the road and at home. The photo by Troy, on one of his many solo rides deep into the Michigan backwoods, called out for a poem. The angle was perfect for the fleeting spirit I wanted to capture. Troy is one of those inspiring persons who feeds my imagination. I acknowledged him in my book. Thanks

Poetry on My Mind," p 51. If you haven't got the book, you're missing out.

ADDENDUM: Note from John Michael Flynn (Carl Sandburg Resident Writer 3/20/19 and Author of " How the Quiet Breathes" and seven other books): Nicely done, Tom. Simple yet profound, much in the vein of many short poems from the Chinese masters such as Li Po. The poem is grounded, not sentimental or false at all, and feels lived. You really cannot ask much more of such a form, and from yourself. In many ways, these are the hardest poems to write. You cannot afford to add one adjective or phrase that doesn't fit the whole. I am reminded of the fine American poet, James Wright. His poem 'Autumn Begins In Martins Ferry, Ohio' is something of a classic in this genre. If you haven't read it, you should check it out. Wright, in general, was a master of the compressed poem, the power to be felt in fewer words rather than more of them. He, too, examined death many times over, and why not? This is what poets do. Another poet you may like, who just left us, is W.S. Merwin. Both of these men were fine poets. We can learn from their bodies of work. I encourage you to keep writing your poems, to keep developing your craft, your skill level with language, your use of metaphor. This will have a positive effect on your non-fiction. You will see your language better as you loosen up, so to speak, to write your prose. I shared your poem with some Turkish colleagues. They really liked it.

THE MAYOR

They call him Mr. Mayor
Oft busks out on the square,
His banjo's like a magnet,
Crowds gathering far to near,
To hear the Mayor's music,
To lean in with every ear.

He picks a tune,
A tune or two,
The gathering joining in,

Clapping and foot stomping,
As the Mayor tickles tin.

The music floats on mountain air,
And skips across the glen
The roll is called on Rocky Top,
By God, the Mayor's in.

TWT, 6/22/2020, Dedicated to Tommy
Beehan

Most people know him as "Mr. Mayor" of Oak Ridge. We went to Father Ryan together and our families knew one another. His Father, Tricky Beehan, earned his nickname as one of Ryan's all-time basketball players. I recall my Father and Tricky were in the first graduating class from Father Ryan High School in 1929. Whoa! That dates us! Although as Oak Ridge's longest standing mayor, Tommy has longer been plinking and strumming the banjo, in bands gone by. His leadership and music echoes through the Smokies and has touched the souls of many a person who came his way. Happy Birthday, Tommy, and many more

FROM THE ASHES

Alone,
In solitude,
In silent contemplation,
Instinctively reverent,
Not a ripple in the great pool,
Where once the Earth trembled,

And ashes lay strewn,
A boy stares at what was,
And asks his Mommy,
Who remembers,
"What can be?"

Author's Note: Where once stood two great towering monuments, symbols of the free and enterprising world, another towering memorial stands now, along with a reflection pool and the names of those who perished. It is a memorial in honor and memory of what happened on that fateful day, 9/11/2001, there on that spot, on our hallowed ground. It is a place where people come together now, that we "never forget" that there is evil in the world and it is our duty to eradicate it with the help of God, in Whom We Trust.

This photo of her son, Canaan, which inspired my late-night poem, was taken by a friend of mine, 9/11/19. Friendships are a beauty of creation. They fill voids in the soul and make us whole. Friendship is the human spirit. The poem is a true story.

Sometimes I write seven poems a week; sometimes I write no poems a week. Poems happen for me. This one summoned up a decade and a generation of smoldering memories - A lone boy by the pool, our future, everyman. Daily I am reminded how fragile Liberty is, and that evil exists in the world and how vigilant we must be. Let us be wary of wolves in sheep's clothing. Let us pray

PROMISES! PROMISES!

We met down on the plains,
It was plain as day to me,
He promised me the moon,
  You see.
Now married,
  We made three.

So all over did I followed him,
Following his dream,
It was a journey far,
For me,
  It seemed.
As I was a home girl from
North Carolina.
Arizona, Oklahoma, Florida,
  Seemed, to me, so far.

But what I discovered,
may surprise you all,
For all the dreams
  And plans you make,
God knows,
Far more than He,
    lets on,
For what I found by following,
Was a happiness so fond!

Finally, finally,
After years of dreams,
For a boat ride,
  He took me,
Not any night it seemed,
For yonder appeared that moon,

I spied,
That moon, he had promised me,
Reaching up nye 24 years,
I plucked what was mine,
        I pinched it from the sky,
The apple of my eye.

My dreams fulfilled,
Promises done,
I plucked the moon,
He promised,
        I'd own.

I just reached up,
Oh look, isn't that neat!
In distant reach,
He laid the moon at my feet.

As I look back on journeys then,
I know they seem haphazardly,
But those moments not,
Would I ever trade,
For here my moment,
Me,
  My moon man,
        and we!
twt 8/17/2020©

SOLITUDE

Solitude is sometimes confused with loneliness
But it is Solitude that fuels the soul
In Solitude we are awakened
In Solitude we begin to appreciate
Solitude recognizes Love
In Solitude we confess our sins
Thoughts in Solitude, thank you Thomas
Solitude is the yen of yang
If a tree falls in Solitude, is it a tree?
Solitude proceeds words and is there when all else fails.
It is in Solitude where we hear ourselves think.
Solitude is to the soul, as Thinking is to the mind
Solitude is where we reflect – It is the quiet time when I realize

really who I am and come face to face with my imperfections
Solitude is patient and impatient
Solitude is the mirror of our existence
Solitude is the quiet before the storm

Listen to the sounds of silence
Solitude reminds me that I have something to tell myself
Be quiet my spirit, if quiet I must be
Be quiet my Spirit and listen to me.
Solitude is a fresh breeze
Solitude is fall leaves
Solitude is the falling snow
Solitude is a fire in the dead of winter
Solitude is a trout stream and no words spoken between kindred friends
Solitude like a thief in the night steals the angry soul
Without Solitude we are nothing, without Solitude we are not I
Solitude Stop – Look - Listen
Solitude is that deafening roar you hear right after you hear bad news
Solitude is the crickets and frogs in the night air
Solitude brings the silent frost that the sun kindly transforms
Shuuu! Quiet.

Solitude is the winged flight of the Owl
Solitude is the quiet before the storm – Solitude is the eye of the storm
Find Solitude and nourish it – Take a cleansing breath and relax.
Solitude is as near as your heart and as far away as the depths of space where
words have not yet reached
Solitude - Turn off the TV, put down the earphones and listen to nothing
Solitude - Read a good book, go fishing, take a hike
Solitude is that moment between prayers
Solitude is nothing and everything at the same time.
Solitude is infinite

Take one minute for yourself
Solitude is inner peace and inner peace must precede outward peace
Without Solitude we cannot proceed
Solitude is the path to the sixth sense

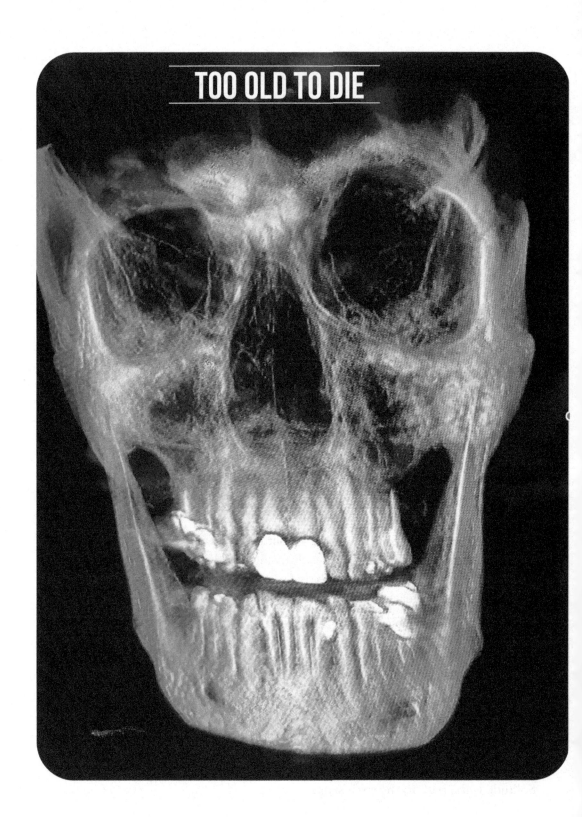
TOO OLD TO DIE

Lord, Dear Lord,
I Pray this day
This prayer I say
Pass me by,
I'm waaay too,
Old to die!

MOON

So open every window,
Throw open every door,
Let the moonlight shower,
Blessings,
Blessings evermore.

I am the moon remember,
Full bright up in your sky,
I was here when you were born,
I'll be here when you die.

I bring you summer solstice,
Your winter solstice too,
I rule your tides at sea,

I quietly spin for you.

I've seen famine, war and
pestilence,
I've seen muslim fighting Jew,
It simply doesn't matter,
Waxing, waning, full or new.

So sleep tight lowly master,
As circle you I do,
For one night I'll come to bid
you,

Alas! your last adieu.

Author's Notes: The Moon from the moon's perspective. Oooo! Goose bumps! The last two lines get real personal, with "chi-bumps" ☺
Kenny Rogers sung, ♪♫♪The best you can hope for is to die in yor sleep♪♫♪

PRINCESS FALLS

There once was a sad waterfall,
Oh my, so dry,
Which required a Princess,
To Climb up upon its rocks,
And declare,
   Aloud,
That it flow, forth,
   Once more.

The rock,
   Suddenly,
As if on command,
Changed to liquid,
   And water fell forth,
     Over that falls
Ten thousand years,
Hence.

There were many faces,
   Frozen,
     In the wall,
From many places indeed,
   Freed,
To welcome her,
   The Princess,
Princess of the Universe.

Author's Note: It takes a free Spirit, a Sprite, to change rock to water. Moses did it once. A bit like the Princess and the frog Prince. True story? Uh! Probably not, but then often fiction, in the form of tales, can be believable, in the eye of the poet. Point well taken. I look at the picture and see faces frozen in stone, waiting for a Princess. Also when I stare at the photo, water begins to flow down that center Vee - You see? You see with your imagination things never before imagined. Look closely at things around you. Look. Listen. Sense. Smell. Taste the cold water. Dare to drink it all in. I dare you.

I see eleven faces. How many do you see?
tom tenbrunsel
poet laureate of my domain   *photo by erin, 6/20/2022*

AS THE WORLD TURNS

As the world turns
Which Way does it turn
clockwise, or
counter clockwise
Would that be wise
If otherwise?
Would that be backward
Or awkward?
Truth be told
What if I were standing on the
South Pole?

What if it didn't turn at all
Or just on Sundays
Then back on Monday
Would it be Tuesday
Saturday or Sunday?
Yesterday?
Perhaps again
Or perhaps Noneday
Or Maby Nonday
Then
When would be my birthday
Or yours
Someday?
Perhaps never?
Never again.

Someday
Perhaps we'll give it a try
Give it a spin
Like the carnival it is
What have we got to lose
Or win?

Some days I wonder
What day it is
It's today
Always today
Silly it's the day before tomorrow
Or the day after yesterday
Or just the next day
today again.

Why does it have to turn
Any way?
Turn turn?
Why not
Stop
At least for a little while
That would be unique
Different
Or eternity
So so many question to speak of
Or not
I'm feeling dizzy!

BIKING ON MY MIND

So there
Then and there
I left my bike,
Grounded
And took a hike.
I looked back and my bike,
Had followed behind.
I'm one with my bike.
My bike I do like.
I have bike,
Biking on my mind!

As along I rode
A riverside ride
The gravel seemed
To talk,
"Crunch crunch"
It said
"You're free
You're free,"
I heard,

My ride,
My ride spoke to me
My ride,
My ride by the stream.

Grinding gravel
On my gravel grinder
Like coursers
My crew and
Me flew.
Gravel beneath,
Above sky blue,
Riding, riding
Round road's bend
My Spirit renewed
I thought
Wher'st will'st -
Where will my
Trail

END?

LOVELY YET LONELY

"Cogitat; ergo est."
Lovely yet lonely
A cold wind blows
A cold statue, it's heart
Within, Bronze gold.

So lovely yet so lonely,
Who placed you here in wrought
With heart of gold in cold cast
Bronze
Your sinews 'gainst the dampness
rot.

Why bitter towards the dampness,
Man with leaden soul?
Is it not enough to spite yourself
To wish you're made of gold?

You're paralyzed to freedom
Your timeless fate is wrought
Though your beauty be
transcendent
Your proud pot steel is not.

Lonely yet so lovely
I shall set you free
Where be you, your desire
Where be that flame and fire?
Give but a rib
A ring I'll make
Transposing cold pot passion
Into white hot pure desire

Destruction to construction,
The fire of my desire.

I'll melt you down and
mold you up
More perfect than before.

In jest why not an answer
In Bessemer forsaking.
Down, damn this prose,
away with sin,
a fusion's in the making.

For corrupt your pride it will
It's nature's freedom fire;
The alchemy of flash-hot flame
Rekindling wrought's desire.

In the suicide of giving,
A new ring of unity,
The ring shall set you free,
This time in Love incorruptible
No cast more perfect there can be.
I shall for you give to my she,
My she a gift of thee.

Author's Note: Originally written circa 1964 and revised in 1996 and again in 2022 before publication. The painting is of Rodin's The Thinker (in the park of the Lindesche Villa with the family in the background) by Edvard Munch is in the public domain.

Art is passion. Fire is passion. Love is passion. The Thinker represents mankind's desire to be, to think, yet to transpose, to resist fixation, to be more. To be other. To pursue. To move about. To transcend. Why was The Thinker not made out of gold? Or was he? Does thinking transcend love?

TWO GENTLEMEN (2)

Poem re-dedicated to my life-long friend, George Aloysius Geist
(3/27/1937 - 8/10/2022) RIP

Two Gentlemen,
Met on Max Patch,
Just a tad,
Below the sky.
Two Gentlemen met
On Max Patch
Hav'n Traveled far and nigh.

One that would,
Talk your ear off,
Tuther,

With big ole' ears,
Their chatter,
And their laughter,
Would bring a body tears,

Of old times,
New times,
Good times,
Of times a' running out,
Next time you see 'em up there,
Give 'em both a shout.

Known each 'chuther forever,
Both with big ole eyes,
Where'd their journeys take 'em,
Under Appalachian skies.

Like brothers to one another,
Brothers-in-laws for sure,
They'd traveled a'ways from Rocky top,
Buena Vista and Howard Road,
They talked about everything from fixing and karting,
They knew bout all'st you need a' know.

Two gentleman,
Met on Max Patch,
Buddies-in-law,
'Bout same age now,
One not the other,
Being older,
Hit don't matter,
Anyhow.

Cause up there on Max Patch,
Just below the stars,
They'd just a soon's meet up there,
Their journeys' who they are.

REQUIEM IN PACE:

The journey to friendship is short and sweet.

I met George when I was a freshman in High School. He married my sister. I am so, so, so glad he married my sister, Ann. He quickly became my best friend in life. So many things we discussed and did and so many things George taught me over the years. What they both taught me was that love is enduring. Love is inseparable. I don't know two people more in love than those two. I don't think they ever spent one day apart and as Al reminded me, they always held hands as they hiked. They both love the Smokey Mountains. I live in the Smokies.

Ann and George built the house they lived in and raised their children together. They maintained their business together. George the genius, could fix anything! Lord, who am I gonna call now when my car makes a strange noise?

Need I remind you that though gone before us, George's Spirit lives on in each one of us. What will I do? Well, for one, I will tell people and write about how I once knew a kind man, a man of faith and love, with a captivating smile and sense of humor, so considerate of others, helpful, smart with an extremely high common-sense IQ, a friend of many. I will tell them he loved his wife and family and God. I will tell them, I knew George Geist, and that we met once or more on Max Patch.

Today, we come together to see George off on his new journey, only to join him later, God willing and to pray in God's name "Requiem in Pace", my friend George. We come also to offer our prayers of support and goodwill to his wife, Ann, he has left behind, my dear and only sister, Ann. Ann, we have you in our prayers too

WISDOM

"Wisdom be not fleeting, but grasp me in thy clutches and set me free, for I am mankind in need!"

Wisdom, what are you?
Where are you?
I grasp for you,
And yet you are fleeting,
As if some fog envelops,
My foggy-wise existence,
So hard to heed,
When best in need!

Show yourself to me, Wisdom.
Pull me from the darkness of desperation,
I cannot think,

I cannot take one step,
Not one desperate step,
Without your lighting my way.
Show me the way,
I beg you, Wisdom
Be with me forever,
And ever, all my days.

Yet is Wisdom fleeting or not?
I rather think not.
The older the wiser?
Perhaps.
    Perhaps not.

Wisdom's unlimited.
Wisdom is free,
So gather Wisdom,
Wherever it may be.
Light this Earth, Wisdom
With your lighted way.
Wisdom is Truth,
Light our days.

Look to your elders.
What They've accrued with age,
Don't write them off,
As your main source of sage.
A bit of advice,
　　Seek out the company,
Of the good and the wise,
Look first for aged sage,
　　In the sage aged,
Where Wisdom's found,
　　Times thrice.

The Wisemen were wise,
Granted, a gift from God,
To follow yon star,
　　Afar.
Though beguiled as fools,
Only to pro-seize the seat of Wisdom,
　　From a Child.

They say you can't take it with you.
Can you?
Do you?
When you die?
Or is Wisdom eternal,
　　Forever,
　　　　Passed on to you from I.

Is Wisdom,
The gold of creation?
And as such,
　shouldn't we clutch,

And cherish,
　And seek it,
　　　In every crevice,
Under every clach?

So heed you not,
Lest Wisdom not,
　Be sought,
　　And forgot,
And pass you by,
　for mere lies.

Seek out the Wise,
And drink in,
Their Wisdom,
　And stories,
　　From within.
For, within, for you,
Tis, a gifted surprise,
No strings attached,
In this U(niverse),
The gold is discovered,
　Within your mind's eye.

For the only way to preserve it,
Wisdom, that is,
Is to hold it within you,
　Let not a day go by,
　　That you don't spy,
Wisdom's wise hue view.

Perhaps it is so,
That Chardin*,
　　Had it discovered,
　　　Indeed,
That Wisdom shared,
Is the Sixth Sense,
　　Uncovered.

Teach your children well,
Lavish them with Wisdom,

Lest they end up knelled,
 Without the key,
  To Heaven

So hear ye! Hear ye!
A word to the wise,
Seize the moment!
Seek out Wisdom,
  From the wise,
Lest the Wise,
 Take it with them,
Leaving you with unknowing,
  Surprise.

Wisdom is the Spirit within us.
So seek Wisdom!

Find Wisdom!
Cherish Wisdom!
Love Wisdom!
Accept Wisdom!
Respect Wisdom!
Honor Wisdom!
Heed Wisdom!

Be wise in your venture!
Pray for Wisdom!

For its Wisdom,
That's God's
Special gift to you.

*Teilhard de Chardin, "A New Synthesis of Evolution." Read It. It's only 72 pages long. It gives insight that the sixth sense is shared intellect/consciousness. Transcend from ignorance. Transcend if you must. Transcend in intellect. Transcend from the dust.
Teilhard prophesied Project Looking Glass, or was he in on its inception.
Wisdom teleports on communication.
I wrote this poem for my grand grandchildren, and they are none the wiser

Speaking words of Wisdom, Let it be. Let it be

HAYDEN'S THEME

She waltzed in, three, quite on her own, dressed so prettily, sat right down, determined, and began to play as if taught by some distant master.

She had neither lesson nor sheet, But she had posture and poise, no ounce of deceit. She had come to Play.

Ivory moved, it was as if the universe had suddenly sorted; It was time to linger, listen, muse, discover, celebrate and enjoy!

Echoed through an empty wooden chamber; "A" a single note rang out, Then another and another, perhaps one more joined in, then others;

Notes began to pour. They melded, flit and flickered, banged and flew; dancing with excitement, filling void with creative musical laughter and delight.

Was it middle "C" or the "B" beginning of a Symphony, "D" or perhaps a Child's Destiny, A destiny to create - Perhaps to paint the soul of Music?"

Love and Beauty composed of a simple score lifted the spirit of her newfound home. Every solitary note filled every corner with Joy as delicate young fingers plied a Rhyming Rhythm from that old box.

The Room came to life as notes appeared out of nowhere, crescendoed, swirled teasingly, flew pleasingly, then faded into memory, hidden now forever in my soul.

Then almost as soon as it had begun, it was over. Was it a Child's Gift? Of course. It was Hayden's Theme to these old ears and tears.

APPALACHIAN UNICORN

"Who?
What thing are you,
I've come upon,
In the woods,
Whilst trekking?
Are you real?
I rather think knot;
Perhaps a fig,
Or figment?
Then there you are,
Each time I pass;
To greet my imagination.
The Trail I take,
To greet you sir;
The Trail is Appalachian."

OH SEA OF GALILEE

Oh take me down
To the Sea of Galillee
Cleanse me
Wash me free
Of my iniquity
For from where I bedded
I woke up amidst a vision
As real as could be
I woke up overlooking
Sunrise over Galilee
My vision of an unearthed
Mount of the Sermon,
Me, Overlooking the Sea
The Sea of Galilee
I Was there to hear His echo
To hear His Word

To feast with the multitude gathered
Loaves and Fishes all around.
There
I was touched and freed
There
At the Sea of Galilee
A donkey's ride away
From destiny
I was freed.
I walked down barefoot
Wadded into the water
And was purified
Blessed
My stress quieted
I tried walking on the water
As did Peter that day
But my faith escaped my
Imaginative hope
Prayer ensued
Hope and Prayer was my alternative.
Could the Spirit
Then
Possibly be the same
As is with me now?
Absolute!
Resolute!
As then
In that Holy Land
Could it be Mother Earth
Blessed by the birth child of Mother
Mary
That watches over us eternally
Are we one with our Maker
One with our Savior
Trust
Faith
Hope
Pray
Spread the Word
Do unto others

Today.
Awakened from my ancient traveled dream
I ask,
No plead
Why then? Why not now?
When mere billions more people
Billions more evil surrounds us
Testing our very Faith
Now needed
Now to hear His word
Now even evermore
On earth
We need it more
Oh rising water of Noah
Cleanse us
Now as before
The Spirit truly abides
In those haunts of yore.
Oh Sea of Galilee
Lift me
Lift me up
Let me walk hand in hand
With He,
He Who set us free!

Aurthor's Note: Is this religious? No. Is it Catholic? No. It is my belief system based on history and science, that there is a Maker in all this. Why does this story never wear out?There is a spiritual side of being human that cannot be set aside, if you struggle with it, pray. Carl Sandburg in his Pulitzer poetic frenzy arrived at the proof of Christ in his poem Silver Star," in the poem, he ends with, "... And a baby there in swaddling clothes, on hay - Why does this story never wear out?"

Think about it. We are still in the time of Christ. In The year 2033 it will be 2000 years since the redeeming death of Christ. Two thousand years ago that day now in the near future. I hope I make it, Aunt Rose, I hope I make it, to celebrate this benchmark of our freedom from oblivion.

Some of my poems are inspired. Some a spirit moves my mind and hand. This poem came direct while in the middle of emailing my son and his wife about their current pilgrimage to the Holy Land. Cold chills moved me to speak my mind. In one of the photos Brian was standing ankle deep on a wooded platform in the actual Sea of Galilee. Hence the reference in the poem.

CAJUN CRISMUS

Yuz'all MERRY CRISMUS WISH fvom all ov' us
Ova' hyear ya hear!
Dis iz de day befo Crismus an' all t'ru my house
Dey ain't nutin hapn'n, not even a damn mouse.
De chirren iez all ova de place -
In Shecarago, Feenix and New Yoark or som'in place.
So's Mamma in her flutie wite gaown,
And i in mee garounteede cap,
I'z gonna selltle em bones down fo'
A long winter nap.
Ain't gonna be no clatter ov dem ole' gators on de lauwn,
Cause i'ma gonna shoot dem basterds ifen' dey do!
So wit a long pole'n stick
And a little flat drover,
I know i'ma g'wana bee a cajun St. Nick.

An' so up de chemin'ie i go,
Out to de flo,
Where i lan' wit' a splat!
(Don't recommin' doin' dat)
An' den turnin wit' a jerk,
Tell em 'gators toe git dem splashing asses on de move, i saiz',
"MERRY CRISMUS to Lisette, (and da yunguns)
"Til' I saw you some mo'!!!"
Ole' Cajun Sanna, by gum

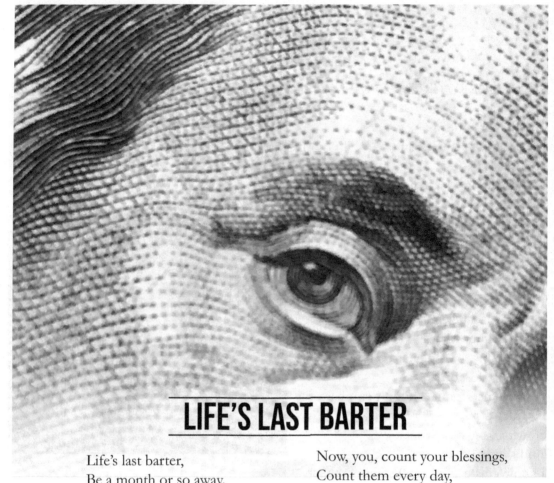

LIFE'S LAST BARTER

Life's last barter,
Be a month or so away.
Yet that carafe to barter,
May come handy any day.

We live life's gift
In a frivolous,
Frivolous sort of way,
Playing to our dis and likes
As though there weren't,
Eternity.

Now, you, count your blessings,
Count them every day,
Live life,
Love and celebrate,
Don't fritter it away,

For the living God
That made you,
On that elusive last day,
Gives you one more chance
To barter,
Eternity away.

Author's Note: Are you ready? Are you prepared? Don't fritter it away. Check in with Jesus. He'll show you the way and hand you your eternal passport, "step this Way."

FOREVER TREKKING

"There are things in my life I never could have imagined"

The Trail begins and ends at the same time and place in forever. Caught only in the moment, bonded hand and hand, they trek along, sharing their adventures, each the reason for each other's existence. (Photo by Erin)

THE CLOCK STRUCK FOURTEEN

Day done, I got ready for bed the same routine as always, late nights. In my comfy PJs, I fluffed up My Giza Pillow, just like Mike does on TV. I even installed a brand new CPAP mask and flung it across the bed in anticipation of crawling deep into my cacoon. No snoring or breathing problems for me. I think I took my nightly meds from the weekly minder snap container. I don't know? The weeks go flashing by, while the days lumber on. Having puffed my inhalers, I tossed the rosary out in the middle of the bed, where I could fish for it in the darkness under two warm cuddly medicinal handmade quilts Just prior to lights out, I checked the security monitor to see all's well for this old man, and whether it was freezing rain or just snowing.

It could be either I thought, it's winter, it's my winter, and winter can be relentless. Sitting on the edge of the bed, in my fav green F16 Tuskegee Airman Alaskan "Fly, Fish, or Flyfish" tee, I was ready for the rollback, duck and cover, of a cold winter's night.As I sat on edge, I noticed a strange quietness, a stillness in the air. I could see my breath! Then without warning, my dear grandmother clock in a distant room began its Westminster symphony, slowly, deliberately, solemnly striking the hour, echoing throughout and empty house. You know how it is you, you count every strike of the clock, bong, bong, bong bong, bong. It's not just the ears that hear, it's the entire body that counts the clock. It was midnight and I counted with grandmother. Ahhh midnight, sweet midnight chimes - 10, 11, 12. But? But? Wait? What? The clock struck 13, then 14! There was that demonstrative 12 chime, then BONG, BONG. I was certain of my body's count. It never failed ... till now. An unrealness, dizzying spell came over me. Strange? Creepy strange. I didn't bother to check the clock. I just drifted off. Stranger still, I never woke up next morning!

Author's Note: Be thee watchful on the watchtower, for you know not the day, nor the hour. You see I probably died before the clock struck maybe during the strikes and the finality of 12 was reassuring. But when the clock went on strike 14, A strange feeling possessed me. I was sure of the strikes and unsure of the hour of death.
Old now, I have looked at myself often. Aging, I've wondered how long I was going to live, I joke with the grandkids and hold my arm up with all those shriveling wrinkles on it, exclaiming, shrieking, startled, "Oh my gosh who is this!" They laugh. I am full of life's journey's joys and wonderful memories. But I knew I was getting old. I know that it is my Winter and I rejoice in having had so many enjoyable seasons. It was time, it was time to go, it was two strokes on the clock passed my midnight. Time got the best of me.For those who have lived a long full life, death comes in "Winter." And when it comes, pray it comes peacefully. I like to think there will be a transition like the transition in the story here. So if, there is indeed a right of passage, a transition, who is writing this review of the midnight hour, in the midnight hour (I'm dead aren't I?)? And wherefrom? From the hereafter? I like to think there is this a period, a transition between life and life after life. I think sometimes we die and don't know it; sometimes die before we know it. We die and sometimes discover we died. So yes, there is likely transition, a passage from life, to life after life. I mean we're still the same person, the same body, soul, mind, spirit - Right? Not having made it through the transition yet, I really can only speculate and you can only guess what's in store. I wish I knew, I can't tell you on faith and hope, what and if there is this peaceful passage between life and life after life after death. I hope there is, if not just tell "Grandmother Clock," fourteen was a good number. You'll just have to find out yourself when your winter comes. Pray before that day and hour

---

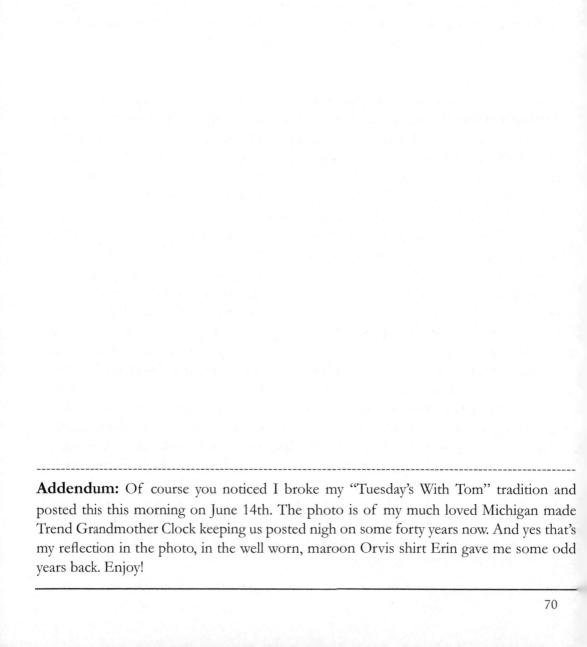

Addendum: Of course you noticed I broke my "Tuesday's With Tom" tradition and posted this this morning on June 14th. The photo is of my much loved Michigan made Trend Grandmother Clock keeping us posted nigh on some forty years now. And yes that's my reflection in the photo, in the well worn, maroon Orvis shirt Erin gave me some odd years back. Enjoy!

THE OLD STORYTELLER FELLER

Along the trail,
A brook and he,
  There he be,
Surprising me,
    By yon tree.
You knew he,
Miles behind him,
Had traveled here

From way aways far,
Perhaps along his way,
  Having logged in every path
And star.

I asked him for
  A story,
A tale perhaps of he.

Along the trail,
A brook and he,
   There he be,
Surprising me,
      By yon tree.
You knew he,
Miles behind him,
Had traveled here
From way aways far,
Perhaps along his way,
   Having logged in every path
And star.

I asked him for
   A story,
A tale perhaps of he.
I asked him to share a bit,
Of life's journey,
   With me.

He told story,
   After story, after story,
      And then more,
Nary one it seemed,
      I'd not heard afore;
Then like that, It dawned!
As he began his stories,
   Even more;
I swear that I had heard them,
I swear I'd heard before.

For he told how he had come,
By hookery
   And crook,
He told me of his journey,
To sit this
   Babbling brook.

Story after story
Turned fire-lit night
   To dawn,
My heart beat fast,
Alas, I now knew;
The storyteller feller,
   "Was You!"

Yes! Yes, by God
I knew, I knew,
I knew, I knew, I knew!
Cause that Storyteller
   Feller,
      You see,
Was my Daddy,
   "He was you."

Many miles behind
   Me now.
As I trek along my way,
My Storyteller, Feller
You see,
   Made me smile
      Each day.

A warm embrace,
Face to time-worn face,
My tear appeared,
   So dear,
To once more hear,
   Your voice,
And a story, more,
   Or two.
"I tell stories too,
Just like you!"

We had trekked along,
Some miles in life,
　　Together, here and there,
　　Him and me,
Missing him so dear,
　　And him so missing me;
He had come back
　　To trek with me
In my latter year -
As I had trekked with he,
For years and years and year.

He's come back,
Thank God,
　　You see,
To see me,
Be with me,
　　Once again,
To trek along beside me,
Toward my story's end.

Author's Note: This is somewhat of a future biography. You see here the bond of parent and child is forever. They did so many things together as they both grew up and old. Dad passed and so did time, albeit all too lonely without each other, but the memories kept them together in the spirit. There is foreboding, hints early on in the poem of what moment this is. Where will you meet your journey's end and who might be there? Will you be doing what you love to do at journey's end? A double negative belays the truth. He appears by "hookery or crook" from where? Did it take some finagling on the other side, from the Boss? Did he hike along a "pathway," a trail, in the "stars," in the heavens? Is he a vision, a ghost, a figment of imagination born out of the strength of emotion - or the energy generated by transition? Is it Teilhard de Chardin's "Sixth Sense," perhaps real in the moment? Perhaps life and life after life intersect? The narrator actually "talks to him." There is so much to say. But they have eternity to share. They "hug." It is real? Of course. Old, older now too was "she" (I did not identify her in the poem, so any reader could define the narrator, but this poem was inspired by a recent camping trip with my daughter, and I know exactly where that meeting takes place), and her daddy came back to be with her, to trek with her, much older now, on her way away. Lifelong, you hold the spirit of those you love. Did she too pass away, that day? Is there life after? Wouldn't it be nice if there were, and it melded with life before, on such occasions. Is there a heaven to trek?

Why do I write of such grief? Because the grief now is part of the happiness then.

The Old Storyteller Feller, from "Poetry on my Mind" by Tom Tenbrunsel, p88

Made in the USA
Coppell, TX
08 June 2024

33273230R00044